AF131423

BOOK ANALYSIS

Written by Maël Tailler and Pauline Coullet

Translated by Soline de Dorlodot and Rebecca Neal

Of Mice and Men

BY JOHN STEINBECK

JOHN STEINBECK

AMERICAN WRITER

- **Born in Salinas (California) in 1902.**
- **Died in New York in 1968.**
- **Notable works:**
  - *Tortilla Flat* (1935), novel
  - *The Grapes of Wrath* (1939), novel
  - *East of Eden* (1952), novel

The American writer John Ernst Steinbeck is best-known for his novels and novellas, which tend to be set in his native California and focus on the difficult living conditions of rural populations. He also worked as a reporter for the *International Herald Tribune* during the Second World War (1939-1945).

In 1962, Steinbeck received the Nobel Prize in Literature for his literary output as a whole. Several of his novels have been adapted for the cinema, and these adaptations have contributed to the popularity of his work.

OF MICE AND MEN

THE ESSENTIAL ANIMALITY OF HUMANKIND

- **Genre:** novella
- **Reference edition:** Steinbeck, J. (2000) *Of Mice and Men*. London: Penguin.
- **1st edition:** 1937
- **Themes:** friendship, dreams, the Great Depression, violence, death, poverty

Of Mice and Men was first published in 1937 and tells the story of Lennie Small, a physically imposing, prodigiously strong man with learning difficulties, and George Milton, a small, quick-witted man, who work together on a ranch in southern California and are inseparable. They dream of saving enough money to buy their own farm and leading a simple life there. However, the world of the ranch is inescapably violent and, although he had no intention of causing any harm, Lennie accidentally kills the wife of the boss's son Curley.

SUMMARY

A NEW JOB

Two seasonal workers, Lennie, a huge man with learning difficulties, and George, a small, intelligent young man, have fled from a ranch in the village of Weed in the north of the United States, and are now wandering through the Californian countryside near Soledad, a remote town in the south. George decides to stop and spend the night by a river and then visit the neighbouring ranch the next morning in the hope of getting some work. This will enable them to earn the money they need to purchase their own farm.

While heating up a can of beans, George warns Lennie that he needs to behave if they want to realise their dream of living on their own farm with their earnings. This means that he needs to stop carrying a dead mouse in his pocket, stay away from girls and, above all, keep quiet. We learn that Lennie had a difficult childhood: he was orphaned at a young age and brought up by a woman named Clara in a small town called

Auburn. Now, he is dependent on George.

The next day, in the ranch's sleeping quarters, they meet an old ranch hand named Candy, the boss and his son Curley, a small, nervous, arrogant man who immediately tries to intimidate them. Once they have left the sleeping quarters, Candy warns them about Curley ("Curley don't take no chances. He always wins", pp. 30-31) and his wife, who has "got the eye" (p. 29). As if to confirm what he says, she comes to meet them, pretending that she is looking for her husband.

George is worried and gives Lennie more advice before Carlson and Slim, two other seasonal workers, come in. Slim's dog has just had puppies and Lennie wants one to stroke. Slim agrees to give him one.

During their breaks, the seasonal workers play at throwing horseshoes as close as possible to a nail; the person who manages to hit the nail wins the game and the money the players have laid down. While the others play, Slim talks with George in the sleeping quarters, and George tells him about Lennie's difficult childhood and their escape from Weed.

Shortly afterwards, Carlson comes in and starts pressuring Candy to kill his dog, which smells and walks with a limp. The old man finally gives in and Carlson leaves with the elderly, ailing animal. At that moment, Curley barges in and tells the workers that he is looking for his wife. Everybody follows him apart from Lennie, Candy and George. When George starts talking about the farm that he and Lennie want to buy, Candy, who is entirely alone in the world, decides to join their venture.

Later on, Curley comes in again and apologises to Slim, who has had enough of his all-consuming jealousy. He then takes out his frustrations on Lennie by provoking and hitting him. Lennie passively accepts the beating, as he does not know what the consequences of fighting back will be, but when George tells him to attack, he crushes Curley's hand. Lennie is frightened, as he fears that now their dream will never come true.

AN IMPOSSIBLE DREAM

On Saturday evening, while George and the others head off to Old Susy's brothel, Lennie goes to the stables where Crooks, the black, disabled groom, sleeps. He cannot hold his tongue and starts talking about their dream, and before long Candy joins them and jumps into the conversation. Crooks is interested, but he does not believe that their dream will ever come true: "Nobody never gets to heaven, and nobody gets no land" (p. 73).

Curley's wife, who is once again pretending to be looking for her husband, arrives and asks what happened to his hand. Candy and Crooks become angry when she starts teasing Lennie and talking about them as if they were common tramps. However, she knows that she is protected by her social status and tells them to be quiet because their opinion does not matter: "Nobody'd listen to you, an' you know it" (p. 80). George comes back and is furious with Lennie for talking about their secret.

Late one afternoon, Lennie remains alone in the stable with a dead puppy while the others play horseshoes. He is trying to hide it, because he is worried that if George finds out, he will not let him look after the rabbits on their farm. Curley's wife comes to talk to him, and although he is initially reluctant, he soon lets himself be drawn into a conversation with her. She confides in him that she wanted to be an actress, but resigned herself to marrying Curley. Lennie tells her that he likes to stroke soft things, and when he wants to touch her hair, she recoils before changing her mind. She sees him as "a big baby" (p. 89), and ends up inviting him to stroke her hair.

However, Lennie begins to stroke her hair increasingly roughly, and when the young woman panics and starts screaming, he sees red. In his attempts to keep her quiet, he accidentally breaks her neck. When Candy and George come in and discover the young woman's lifeless body, they know that their dream is over, as they immediately realise that Lennie has killed her and that Curley will want to lynch him. George then goes to steal Carlson's gun and pretends to arrive at the scene at the same time as Curley and the others, who have just discovered the body. In spite of George's efforts to calm Curley down and save his friend, he will not be reasoned with, and Lennie is sentenced to death.

Lennie goes back to the riverbank, as George had told him to do if things went wrong. He feels guilty and imagines that his aunt and a giant rabbit have come to scold him. George finds him and comforts him by talking about their farm and telling him that it was not his fault. However, at the same time he gets the gun out and, reluctantly, with a trembling hand, shoots his friend in the neck. When the others arrive, they see Lennie's body next to George, who is sitting "stiffly" (p. 105) by the river in silence. Slim goes over to him and suggests that he come have a drink with them. Curley and Carlson do not understand their pain.

CHARACTER STUDY

The novel's straightforward structure and plot make it easy to rank the characters based on the amount of power they have, which governs their attitudes and behaviour. From most to least powerful, we have:

THE BOSS

The boss is a small, stocky man who does not care about his employees, as long as they work. He represents authority, but only appears once in the story.

CURLEY

Like his father, to whom he owes his power, Curley's clothes set him apart from the seasonal workers: he wears boots with high heels and a glove full of Vaseline on his left hand to keep it "soft for his wife" (p. 29).

He has a marked jealous streak, enjoys provoking other people, and spends his time reminding the seasonal workers of his status and running after his wife. He is arrogant, vain and insensitive, and has something of a complex about his small stature: Candy tells George and Lennie that he "hates big guys" (p. 28). He sometimes tries to use violence to assert his power (he is a lightweight boxer), but everyone sees through his posturing and he never really establishes his authority over men of character.

CURLEY'S WIFE

We are never told Curley's wife's name. She is vulgar and uncouth, but knows how to attract attention: she behaves provocatively, wears heavy make-up and passes the time by flirting with the seasonal workers. Beneath this veneer, she is bitter and lonely: she wanted to be a Hollywood actress, but settled for marrying Curley because nobody better came along. She does not love her husband, and as soon as his back is turned, she looks for other people to keep her company or uses her higher social status to humiliate those weaker than her, particularly Crooks and Candy.

When she finds herself alone with Lennie, his strange but kind appearance inspires her to confide in him. When he asks to stroke her hair, she lets him, not only as a reward for listening to her, but also because she is proud of her silky hair. However, Lennie is too rough with her and accidentally breaks her neck.

THE SEASONAL WORKERS

The seasonal workers are simple men who all wear "blue jeans and a short denim jacket" (p. 34). They tend to be single, and work very hard to earn a few dollars per week, which they spend at the weekends on alcohol and girls to "get ever'thing outta [their] system" (p. 56). They all dream of a better life, but their harsh living conditions make this impossible.

Their power is relative and short-lived, and comes from sticking together: for example, Candy and Crooks manage to preserve their dignity by briefly standing firm against Curley's wife. However, although they feel a natural affection for one another, their individualism and their fear of losing their jobs force each of them to distrust and keep their distance from the others.

The seasonal workers are central to the novel, and can be divided into two groups:

The strongest

- **George Milton** is "small and quick, dark of face, with restless eyes and sharp, strong features" (p. 4). He and Lennie are the story's two main characters. George is an intelligent, honest, spontaneous and generous man who took Lennie under his wing after the woman who raised him died. Although the two men are different in many ways, they complement one another and form a strong alliance: George's quick mind and Lennie's prodigious strength are both essential to their survival. George's surname is a reference to one of Steinbeck's literary inspirations, the English poet John Milton (1608-1674), whose epic poem *Paradise Lost* is about the fall of man and therefore echoes George and Lennie's story.
- **Carlson** is a strong, well-built man. When he decides to kill Candy's dog, nobody dares to challenge him.
- **Slim**, the ranch's skinner, is a kind man with a deep voice who is universally respected. He is

the person who really runs the ranch.
- **Whit** is the youngest man on the farm, but already walks with a stoop because of his work.

The weakest

- **Lennie Small** is George's opposite in terms of physical appearance: he is "a huge man, shapeless of face, with large, pale eyes, and wide, sloping shoulders" (p. 4). He is physically imposing, mentally disabled and kind-hearted, and is often compared to an animal ("he walked heavily, dragging his feet a little, the way a bear drags his paws", *ibid.*) or a child ("Sure he's jes' like a kid", p. 44). He is innocent, clumsy, sensitive and unintelligent, and relies on George because he is incapable of living independently. He is undeniably the strongest man on the ranch, physically speaking, but his naivety and lack of intelligence often leave him vulnerable (George is clearly the dominant figure in their friendship and blames him for all their problems; Curley takes out his anger on him). His surname contrasts with his strength and hints at his fundamental weakness.

- **Candy** is an old man with a white beard who has been worn down by life. He lost his left hand while working, which means that he can now only carry out household chores, and he is too old to accompany the others when they go into town. He is afraid of dying alone because he knows that when he becomes a burden, he will not be put out of his misery like Carlson did for his dog.
- **Crooks**, the black, disabled groom, is right at the bottom of the ranch's hierarchy. Because of his race, he is viewed as inferior and ostracised: he is the only one to sleep in the stables, where no other seasonal worker goes (Lennie is the first to do so), nobody talks to him and the other men refuse to let him join their card games, claiming that he smells. However, he is the best at throwing horseshoes and the only one who reads books.

ANALYSIS

STEINBECK AND HIS TIME

The Great Depression

Although George and Lennie's story is fictional, the Great Depression which forms the backdrop to it was real, and was the most serious economic crisis of the 20th century. It was triggered by the Wall Street Crash on 24 October 1929, which plunged much of the world into a decade-long recession. In the USA, this period saw skyrocketing unemployment, rising poverty and profound social and economic change.

American farmers were hit particularly hard by the crisis, as the Great Depression caused crop prices to plummet and led to a 60% drop in agricultural production. Many farmers were ruined and lost their farms.

These difficult conditions were exacerbated by an unprecedented natural disaster known as the Dust Bowl. This was a period of severe drought and dust storms that affected the Great Plains running down the centre of the USA. This destroyed harvests and, coupled with the effects of the Great Depression, was enough to drive many small farmers to ruin.

Farmworkers were forced to leave their land and head to California, which was seen as a "promised land" because of its temperate climate and thriving fruit and vegetable farms. Steinbeck focused closely on this exodus, which brought over a million farmers to California in the 1930s, in his most famous novel, *The Grapes of Wrath*. This vast workforce made it possible for owners to considerably reduce wages, forcing farmers into poverty. This meant that during the Great Depression, farmworkers often fell prey to the same pessimism and fatalism exhibited by the characters in *Of Mice and Men*.

The economic crisis and exodus of farmworkers form the backdrop to the story. George and Lennie's story illustrates the hardships faced by these itinerant workers and the dream that many of them shared: to find a job and earn enough money to ensure their independence.

Behaviourism

Behaviourism is a branch of psychology which was developed in the USA in the early 20th century by the psychologist John Broadus Watson (1878-1958) and which involves observing human behaviour objectively. It is a form of behavioural psychology, and behaviourists believe that the best way to analyse an individual's mental state is not to examine their thoughts and feelings, but rather to consider their outward behaviour and attitude.

Many authors in the early 20th century, including Steinbeck, were influenced by behaviourism. It plays a key role in the majority of his novels, which also stand out for their realism: he describes his characters' behaviour with considerable precision and objectivity, and the third-person narrator recounts the events of the story with total impartiality. We learn about the characters through their conversations and objective descriptions. A striking example of this comes at the beginning of the novel, when we are introduced to George and Lennie for the first time. We are not given any insight into their thoughts, so it is impossible for us to tell who they are or what they are thinking, but we gain an understanding of their key personality traits by the way that they are described.

When we first encounter George and Lennie, they are walking "in single file" (p. 4), with George, the more dominant of the two men, leading the way. He comes across as dynamic and confident ("Every part of him was defined", *ibid.*), and his "restless eyes and sharp strong features" (*ibid.*) give the impression that his life has not been an easy one. Conversely, Lennie appears to be a meeker character: he follows George, seemingly without knowing or caring where they are going, and has a "shapeless" face and "sloping shoulders" (*ibid.*). He "walk[s] heavily, dragging his feet a little" and his arms "[do] not swing at his sides, but [hang] loosely" (*ibid.*). Steinbeck employs a very "visual" writing style for this description.

We are not given any details about the two protagonists' past or personality, but this description of their behaviour instantly gives us an idea of what they are like. Similarly, when the two friends first meet Curley, he adopts an intimidating stance: "His arms gradually bent at the elbows and his hands closed into fists.

He stiffened and went into a slight crouch. His glance was at once calculating and pugnacious" (p. 27). The narrator does not explicitly say that Curley is arrogant and distrustful, but his tense, aggressive posture and hostile gaze speak volumes about his personality.

Even though the narrator remains objective and we have no insight into the characters' thoughts, the text is far from devoid of emotion. For example, the contrast between the poetic, visual descriptions and the short, incisive dialogue reflects George and Lennie's ambiguous relationship, which seems at once rough and tender. In spite of George's claims to the contrary (at the start of the novel, he says that he would be better off without Lennie), their friendship is very strong. The fact that the other characters, such as Candy and Crooks, are utterly alone throws their relationship into even sharper relief.

HUMANITY AND ANIMALITY

The novel's title is inspired by a fragment from the Scottish poet Robert Burns's (1757-1796) poem "To a Mouse": "The best-laid schemes o' mice an' men/Gang aft agley" (often paraphrased in

English as "the best-laid plans of mice and men often go awry"). This title suggests that humans and animals are fundamentally similar (an impression which is strengthened by the alliteration of "mice" and "men", which symbolically unites the two species) and that, in spite of our pretentions, we are still all animals deep down.

This comparison recurs throughout the novel:

- Lennie's appearance, lack of intelligence and impulsiveness inspire the narrator to compare him to a bear (pp. 4 and 98), a horse (p. 4) and a dog (p. 71);
- the men are often likened to dogs, rats (George describes Curley's wife as "a rattrap if I ever seen one", p. 34) and rabbits;
- women are often compared to hens or to chickens (p. 78).

Two of the novel's subplots reinforce this parallel:

- Slim's puppies. Slim is forced to kill off the weakest half of his litter of puppies so that the others can survive. Furthermore, Curley's wife's body lies on the floor of the stable next to the puppy that Lenny accidentally killed.

- Candy's senile old dog. Like his four-legged companion, Candy limps around the ranch, but will not be put out of his misery when he starts being a burden to the others. Crooks is ostracised because the other men say he smells (he sleeps in the stables, away from the other men), but it is the dog's smell that drives Carlson to kill him. Crooks is therefore implicitly compared to a dog.

FORESHADOWING IN THE NOVEL

Several elements foreshadow the novel's tragic ending. This narrative determinism conveys a pessimistic outlook on the world, but a glimmer of hope still remains.

Until late on in the story, the reader is encouraged to believe that George and Lennie's dream could still come true. Although Lennie repeatedly breaks his promise to keep quiet about their plans, the more he talks, the more people seem to rally to their dream, the more their future community grows, and the more this dream seems to become reality. The reader is therefore invited to hope with them, and the novel makes it seem as though George and Lennie could escape the fate of their fellow farmworkers.

However, there are a number of clues that hint at the novel's tragic ending:

- **The title**. Readers who are familiar with Burns's poem will know that it is pessimistic.
- **The novel's characters and the world it depicts**, which is characterised by violence, poverty and individualism. These create a chain of oppression which will inevitably end up breaking one of its links. George and Lennie's friendship is an exception to this rule, and it is significant that it is broken from the inside: George kills Lennie, but he could have run away with him.
- **George's surname** (Milton). This intertextual reference hints that the farm the protagonists dream of buying is also a "paradise lost".
- **Lennie**, who inadvertently causes harm and is repeatedly warned about his behaviour by the other characters, particularly George. The rules he must follow seem simple enough: he has to keep quiet, avoid women and be careful with weaker creatures (such as the puppies). However, his size, power and impulsiveness make it impossible for him to obey the rules.

Towards the beginning of the novel, we learn that he caused problems on the ranch in Weed, where he lived in a community with other men. Over time, his inappropriate behaviour has increasingly serious consequences: he kills a mouse, then a puppy, then a woman, before being killed himself.

- On a textual level, there are some **seemingly prophetic passages**:
  - ◦ The darkness that gradually permeates the stable towards the end of the novel foreshadows a tragic event (Curley's wife's death, which puts an end to Lennie's dream).
  - ◦ If the description of the area around the river is compared to the beginning of the novel, it foreshadows the novel's ending. Initially, George and Lennie's natural surroundings seem calm and harmonious, and numerous descriptions reinforce this impression: "willows fresh and green with every spring" (p. 3); "a path beaten hard by boys coming down from the ranches to swim in the deep pool" (*ibid*.), etc. By the end of the novel, this setting has changed, as harmony between species has given way to a violent struggle (a heron eats a snake before being driven

away by Lennie) and dormant life has been replaced by peaceful death: "a pleasant shade had fallen", "brown, dry leaves on the ground" "And row on row of tiny wind waves flowed up the green pool" (p. 98).

The novel therefore contains numerous hints that its characters will meet a tragic end. It constitutes a metaphor for a society in which everyone has dreams that will never come true.

A THEATRICAL NOVEL

Of Mice and Men was an immediate success when it was published in 1937, and the director George S. Kaufman (1889-1961) soon suggested a Broadway adaptation to Steinbeck. This play was also a hit, with 207 performances and the 1938 Best Play award from the New York Drama Critics' Circle.

The success of this adaptation is unsurprising, given that *Of Mice and Men* is a hybrid work with features of both the novel and the play: although it takes the form of a novel, its structure means that it can be adapted for the stage with minimal changes. One critic even went so far as to refer to the book as a "play-novelette".

The novel's hybridity can be clearly seen in the form of its narration. As Steinbeck uses an objective third-person narrator, the reader steps into the role of spectator and watches the events unfold as if the book were a play. There is also a significant amount of dialogue, accompanied by sections of narrative that are so brief that they resemble stage directions. The scene in which we are introduced to Curley's wife, who immediately adopts a flirtatious pose, perfectly illustrates this approach:

> "'Oh!' She put her hands behind her back and leaned against the door frame so that her body was thrown forward.
> 'You're the new fellows that just come, ain't ya?
> 'Yeah.'
> Lennie's eyes moved down over her body, and though she did not seem to be looking at Lennie she bridled a little. She looked at her fingernails. 'Sometimes Curley's in here,' she explained. [...] She smiled archly and twitched her body. 'Nobody can't blame a person for lookin'' she said. There were footsteps behind her, going by. She turned her head." (pp. 32-33)

Furthermore, the novel observes two of the three unities of classical theatre, namely unity of place (the entire story unfolds on the ranch) and unity of action (the story features one main plot, namely the gradual demise of George and Lennie's dream). However, the unity of time is not respected: while this rule states that the plot of a play must take place over no more than 24 hours, the events of the novel unfold over the course of three days. Finally, the story has both the density and the sense of determinism of a classical play, as the novel's tragic ending is foreshadowed from the beginning, with Steinbeck dropping an increasing number of hints about the impending disaster (the deaths of Curley's wife and Lennie).

No matter what they do, the characters are doomed, and although they are full of hope at the start of the novel, they soon realise that they cannot outrun their destiny: their paradise is lost, and Lennie's good intentions are not enough to save him from the problems he causes.

Of Mice and Men is above all the story of the two main characters' unshakeable friendship, whose power stems from its simplicity and the difficult circumstances in which it was forged. The novel's strength lies in its emotional resonance, which makes it an undeniable classic of American literature.

FURTHER REFLECTION

SOME QUESTIONS TO THINK ABOUT...

- Explain the novel's title.
- What do the physical descriptions of the novel's characters reveal about their personalities?
- How does the novel depict women? Is this the same as in Steinbeck's other works?
- Identify and explain the comparisons between humans and animals that recur throughout the novel.
- How does the novel reflect the historical context in which it was written (the 1930s)?
- In your opinion, is Steinbeck's portrayal of the human condition optimistic or pessimistic? Explain your answer.
- Why did George and Lennie decide to leave the ranch in Weed?
- Several elements allude to the work's tragic ending. What are they?
- In your opinion, why does George kill Lennie at the end of the novel?

- Outline the main differences between George and Lennie.

We want to hear from you!
Leave a comment on your online library
and share your favourite books on social media!

FURTHER READING

REFERENCE EDITION

- Steinbeck, J. (2000) *Of Mice and Men*. London: Penguin.

ADAPTATIONS

- Steinbeck, J. (1937) *Of Mice and Men* (play). First performance at the Music Box Theatre, Broadway in 1937.

- *Of Mice and Men.* (1939) [Film]. Lewis Milestone. Dir. USA: Hal Roach Studios.

- Floyd, C. (1969) *Of Mice and Men* (opera). First performed by the Seattle Opera in 1970.

- *Of Mice and Men.* (1992) [Film]. Gary Sinise. Dir. USA: Metro-Goldwyn-Mayer (MGM).

MORE FROM BRIGHTSUMMARIES.COM

- Reading guide – *The Grapes of Wrath* by John Steinbeck.

- Reading guide – *The Pearl* by John Steinbeck.

www.brightsummaries.com

Ebook EAN: 9782806270573

Paperback EAN: 9782806274175

Legal Deposit: D/2015/12603/625

This guide was written with the collaboration of Pauline Coullet and translated with the collaboration of Rebecca Neal for the character study of Curley's wife, and for the sections "Steinbeck and his time" and "A theatrical novel".

Cover: © Primento

Digital conception by Primento, the digital partner of publishers.